ALSO BY LOUISE GLÜCK

WINTER RECIPES

FROM THE COLLECTIVE

WINTER RECIPES
FROM THE COLLECTIVE

LOUISE GLÜCK

Farrar, Straus and Giroux • New York

Farrar, Straus and Giroux
120 Broadway, New York 10271

Printed in the United States of America
Published in 2021 by Farrar, Straus and Giroux
First paperback edition, 2022

The Library of Congress has cataloged the hardcover edition as follows:
Names: Glück, Louise, 1943– author.
Title: Winter recipes from the collective / Louise Glück.
Description: First edition. | New York : Farrar, Straus and Giroux, 2021.
Identifiers: LCCN 2021021485 | ISBN 9780374604103 (hardcover)
Subjects: LCGFT: Poetry.
Classification: LCC PS3557.L8 W56 2021 | DDC 811/.54—dc23
LC record available at https://lccn.loc.gov/2021021485

Paperback ISBN: 9780374606480

Designed by Gretchen Achilles

Our books may be purchased in bulk for promotional,
educational, or business use. Please contact your local bookseller
or the Macmillan Corporate and Premium Sales Department
at 1-800-221-7945, extension 5442, or by email at
MacmillanSpecialMarkets@macmillan.com.

www.fsgbooks.com
www.twitter.com/fsgbooks • www.facebook.com/fsgbooks

10 9 8 7 6 5 4 3

For Kathryn Davis

CONTENTS

WINTER RECIPES

FROM THE COLLECTIVE

POEM

Day and night come
hand in hand like a boy and a girl
pausing only to eat wild berries out of a dish
painted with pictures of birds.

They climb the high ice-covered mountain,
then they fly away. But you and I
don't do such things—

We climb the same mountain;
I say a prayer for the wind to lift us
but it does no good;
you hide your head so as not
to see the end—

Downward and downward and downward and downward
is where the wind is taking us;

I try to comfort you
but words are not the answer;
I sing to you as mother sang to me—

Your eyes are closed. We pass
the boy and girl we saw at the beginning;
now they are standing on a wooden bridge;
I can see their house behind them;

How fast you go they call to us,
but no, the wind is in our ears,
that is what we hear—

And then we are simply falling—

And the world goes by,
all the worlds, each more beautiful than the last;

I touch your cheek to protect you—

THE DENIAL OF DEATH

I. A TRAVEL DIARY

I had left my passport at an inn we stayed at for a night or so
whose name I couldn't remember. This is how it began.
The next hotel would not receive me,
a beautiful hotel, in an orange grove, with a view of the sea.
How casually you accepted
the room that would have been ours,
and, later, how merrily you stood on the balcony,
pelting me with foil-wrapped chocolates. The next day
you resumed the journey we would have taken together.

The concierge procured an old blanket for me.
By day, I sat outside the kitchen. By night, I spread my blanket
among the orange trees. Every day the same, except for the weather.

After a time, the staff took pity on me.
The busboy would bring me food from the evening meal,
the odd potato or bit of lamb. Sometimes a postcard arrived.
On the front, glossy landmarks and works of art.
Once, a mountain covered in snow. After a month or so,
there was a postscript: *X sends regards.*

I say a month, but really I had no idea of time.
The busboy disappeared. There was a new busboy, then one more, I believe.
From time to time, one would join me on my blanket.

I loved those days! each one exactly like its predecessor.
There were the stone steps we climbed together
and the little town where we breakfasted. Very far away,
I could see the cove where we used to swim, but not hear anymore
the children calling out to one another, nor hear
you anymore, asking me if I would like a cold drink,
which I always would.

When the postcards stopped, I read the old ones again.
I saw myself standing under the balcony in that rain
of foil-covered kisses, unable to believe you would abandon me,
begging you, of course, though not in words—

The concierge, I realized, had been standing beside me.
Do not be sad, he said. You have begun your own journey,
not into the world, like your friend's, but into yourself and your memories.
As they fall away, perhaps you will attain
that enviable emptiness into which
all things flow, like the empty cup in the Daodejing—

Everything is change, he said, and everything is connected.
Also everything returns, but what returns is not
what went away—

We watched you walk away. Down the stone steps
and into the little town. I felt
something true had been spoken
and though I would have preferred to have spoken it myself
I was glad at least to have heard it.

2. THE STORY OF THE PASSPORT

It came back but you did not come back.
It happened as follows:

One day an envelope arrived,
bearing stamps from a small European republic.
This the concierge handed me with an air of great ceremony;
I tried to open it in the same spirit.

Inside was my passport.
There was my face, or what had been my face
at some point, deep in the past.
But I had parted ways with it,
that face smiling with such conviction,
filled with all the memories of our travels together
and our dreams of other journeys—

I threw it into the sea.

It sank immediately.
Downward, downward, while I continued
staring into the empty water.

All this time the concierge was watching me.
Come, he said, taking my arm. And we began
to walk around the lake, as was my daily habit.

I see, he said, that you no longer
wish to resume your former life,
to move, that is, in a straight line as time
suggests we do, but rather (here he gestured toward the lake)
in a circle which aspires to
that stillness at the heart of things,
though I prefer to think it also resembles a clock.

Here he took out of his pocket
the large watch that was always with him. I challenge you, he said,
to tell, looking at this, if it is Monday or Tuesday.
But if you look at the hand that holds it, you will realize I am not
a young man anymore, my hair is silver.
Nor will you be surprised to learn
it was once dark, as yours must have been dark,
and curly, I would say.

Through this recital, we were both
watching a group of children playing in the shallows,
each body circled by a rubber tube.
Red and blue, green and yellow,
a rainbow of children splashing in the clear lake.

I could hear the clock ticking,
presumably alluding to the passage of time
while in fact annulling it.

You must ask yourself, he said, if you deceive yourself.
By which I mean looking at the watch and not
the hand holding it. We stood awhile, staring at the lake,
each of us thinking our own thoughts.

But isn't the life of the philosopher
exactly as you describe, I said. Going over the same course,
waiting for truth to disclose itself.

But you have stopped making things, he said, which is what
the philosopher does. Remember when you kept what you called
your travel journal? You used to read it to me,
I remember it was filled with stories of every kind,
mostly love stories and stories about loss, punctuated
with fantastic details such as wouldn't occur to most of us,

and yet hearing them I had a sense I was listening
to my own experience but more beautifully related
than I could ever have done. I felt

you were talking to me or about me though I never left your side.
What was it called? A travel diary, I think you said,
though I often called it *The Denial of Death*, after Ernest Becker.
And you had an odd name for me, I remember.

Concierge, I said. *Concierge* is what I called you.
And before that, *you*, which is, I believe,
a convention in fiction.

WINTER RECIPES FROM THE COLLECTIVE

I.

Each year when winter came, the old men entered
the woods to gather the moss that grew
on the north side of certain junipers.
It was slow work, taking many days, though these
were short days because the light was waning,
and when their packs were full, painfully
they made their way home, moss being heavy to carry.
The wives fermented these mosses, a time-consuming project
especially for people so old
they had been born in another century.
But they had patience, these elderly men and women,
such as you and I can hardly imagine,
and when the moss was cured, it was with wild mustards and sturdy herbs
packed between the halves of ciabattine, and weighted like pan bagnat,
after which the thing was done: an "invigorating winter sandwich"
it was called, but no one said
it was good to eat; it was what you ate
when there was nothing else, like matzoh in the desert, which
our parents called the bread of affliction— Some years
an old man would not return from the woods, and then his wife would need
a new life, as a nurse's helper, or to supervise
the young people who did the heavy work, or to sell

the sandwiches in the open market as the snow fell, wrapped
in wax paper— The book contains
only recipes for winter, when life is hard. In spring,
anyone can make a fine meal.

2.

Of the moss, the prettiest was saved
for bonsai, for which
a small room had been designated,
though few of us had the gift,
and even then a long apprenticeship
was necessary, the rules being complicated.
A bright light shone on the specimen being pruned,
never into animal shapes, which were frowned on,
only into those shapes
natural to the species— Those of us who watched
sometimes chose the container, in my case
a porcelain bowl, given me by my grandmother.
The wind grew harsher around us.
Under the bright light, my friend
who was shaping the tree set down her shears.
The tree seemed beautiful to me,
not finished perhaps, still it was beautiful, the moss
draped around its roots— I was not
permitted to prune it but I held the bowl in my hands,
a pine blowing in high wind
like man in the universe.

3 .

As I said, the work was hard—
not simply caring for the little trees
but caring for ourselves as well,
feeding ourselves, cleaning the public rooms—
But the trees were everything.
And how sad we were when one died,
and they do die, despite having been
removed from nature; all things die eventually.
I minded most with the ones that lost their leaves,
which would pile up on the moss and stones—
The trees were miniature, as I have said,
but there is no such thing as death in miniature.
Shadows passing over the snow,
steps approaching and going away.
The dead leaves lay on the stones;
there was no wind to lift them.

4 ·

It was as dark as it would ever be
but then I knew to expect this,
the month being December, the month of darkness.
It was early morning. I was walking
from my room to the arboretum; for obvious reasons,
we were encouraged never to be alone,
but exceptions were made— I could see
the arboretum glowing across the snow;
the trees had been hung with tiny lights,
I remember thinking how they must be
visible from far away, not that we went, mainly,
far away— Everything was still.
In the kitchen, sandwiches were being wrapped for market.
My friend used to do this work.
Huli songli, our instructor called her,
giver of care. I remember
watching her: inside the door,
procedures written on a card in Chinese characters
translated as *the same things in the same order*,
and underneath: *We have deprived them of their origins,*
they have come to need us now.

WINTER JOURNEY

Well, it was just as I thought,
the path
all but obliterated—

We had moved then
from the first to the second stage,
from the dream to the proposition.
And look—

here is the line between,
resembling
this line from which our words emerge;
moonlight breaks through.

Shadows on the snow
cast by pine trees.

•

Say goodbye to standing up,
my sister said. We were sitting on our favorite bench
outside the common room, having
a glass of gin without ice.
Looked a lot like water, so the nurses
smiled at you as they passed,
pleased with how hydrated you were becoming.

Inside the common room, the advanced cases
were watching television under a sign that said
Welcome to Happy Hour.
If you can't read, my sister said,
can you be happy?

We were having a fine old time getting old,
everything hunky-dory as the nurses said,

though you could tell
snow was beginning to fall,
not fall exactly, more like weave side to side,
sliding around in the sky—

.

Now we are home, my mother said;
before, we were at Aunt Posy's.
And, between, in the car, the Pontiac,
driving from Hewlett to Woodmere.
You children, my mother said, must sleep
as much as possible. Lights
were shining in the trees:
those are the stars, my mother said.
Then I was in my bed. How could the stars be there
when there were no trees?
On the ceiling, silly, that's where they were.

·

I must say
I was very tired walking along the road,
very tired— I put my hat on a snowbank.

Even then I was not light enough,
my body a burden to me.

Along the path, there were
things that had died along the way—

lumps of snow,
that's what they were—

The wind blew. Nights I could see
shadows of the pines, the moon
was that bright.

Every hour or so, my friend turned to wave at me,
or I believed she did, though
the dark obscured her.
Still her presence sustained me:
some of you will know what I mean.

ꜛ

NIGHT THOUGHTS

Long ago I was born.
There is no one alive anymore
who remembers me as a baby.
Was I a good baby? A
bad? Except in my head
that debate is now
silenced forever.
What constitutes
a bad baby, I wondered. Colic,
my mother said, which meant
it cried a lot.
What harm could there be
in that? How hard it was
to be alive, no wonder
they all died. And how small
I must have been, suspended
in my mother, being patted by her
approvingly.
What a shame I became
verbal, with no connection
to that memory. My mother's love!
All too soon I emerged
my true self,
robust but sour,
like an alarm clock.

AN ENDLESS STORY

I .

Halfway through the sentence
she fell asleep. She had been telling
some sort of fable concerning
a young girl who wakens one morning
as a bird. So like life,
said the person next to me. I wonder,
he went on, do you suppose our friend here
plans to fly away when she wakens?
The room was very quiet.
We were both studying her; in fact,
everyone in the room was studying her.
To me, she seemed as before, though
her head was slumped on her chest; still,
her color was good— She seems to be breathing,
my neighbor said. Not only that, he went on,
we are all of us in this room breathing—
just how you want a story to end. And yet,
he added, we may never know
whether the story was intended to be
a cautionary tale or perhaps a love story,
since it has been interrupted. So we cannot be certain
we have as yet experienced the end.
But who does, he said. Who does?

2.

We stayed like this a long time,
stranded, I thought to myself,
like ships paralyzed by bad weather.
My neighbor had withdrawn into himself.
Something, I felt, existed between us,
nothing so final as a baby,
but real nevertheless—
Meanwhile, no one spoke.
No one rushed to get help
or knelt beside the prone woman.
The sun was going down; long shadows of the elms
spread like dark lakes over the grass.
Finally my neighbor raised his head.
Clearly, he said, someone must finish this story
which was, I believe, to have been
a love story such as silly women tell, meaning
very long, filled with tangents and distractions
meant to disguise the fundamental
tedium of its simplicities. But as, he said,
we have changed riders, we may as well change
horses at the same time. Now that the tale is mine,
I prefer that it be a meditation on existence.
The room grew very still.

I know what you think, he said; we all despise
stories that seem dry and interminable, but mine
will be a true love story,
if by love we mean the way we loved when we were young,
as though there were no time at all.

3 ·

Soon night fell. Automatically
the lights came on.
On the floor, the woman moved.
Someone had covered her with a blanket
which she thrust aside.
Is it morning, she said. She had
propped herself up somehow so she could see
the door. There was a bird, she said.
Someone is supposed to kiss it.
Perhaps it has been kissed already, my neighbor said.
Oh no, she said. Once it is kissed
it becomes a human being. So it cannot fly;
it can only sit and stand and lie down.
And kiss, my neighbor waggishly added.
Not anymore, she said. There was just the one time
to break the spell that had frozen its heart.
That was a bad trade, she said,
the wings for the kiss.
She gazed at us, like a figure on top of a mountain
looking down, though we were the ones looking down,
in actual fact. Obviously my mind is not what it was, she said.
Most of my facts have disappeared, but certain
underlying principles have been in consequence
exposed with surprising clarity.

The Chinese were right, she said, to revere the old.
Look at us, she said. We are all of us in this room
still waiting to be transformed. This is why we search for love.
We search for it all of our lives,
even after we find it.

PRESIDENTS' DAY

Lots of good-natured sunshine everywhere
making the snow glitter   quite
lifelike, I thought, nice
to see that again; my hands
were almost warm. Some
principle is at work, I thought:
commendable, taking an interest
in human life, but to be safe
I threw some snow over my shoulder,
since I had no salt. And sure enough
the clouds came back, and sure enough
the sky grew dark and menacing,
all as before, except
the losses were piling up—
And yet, moments ago
the sun was shining. How joyful my head was,
basking in it, getting to feel it first
while the limbs waited. Like a deserted hive.
Joyful—now there's a word
we haven't used in a while.

AUTUMN

The part of life
devoted to contemplation
was at odds with the part
committed to action.

.

Fall was approaching.
But I remember
it was always approaching
once school ended.

.

Life, my sister said,
is like a torch passed now
from the body to the mind.
Sadly, she went on, the mind is not
there to receive it.

The sun was setting.
Ah, the torch, she said.
It has gone out, I believe.
Our best hope is that it's flickering,
fort/da, fort/da, like little Ernst
throwing his toy over the side of his crib
and then pulling it back. It's too bad,
she said, there are no children here.
We could learn from them, as Freud did.

·

We would sometimes sit
on benches outside the dining room.
The smell of leaves burning.

Old people and fire, she said.
Not a good thing. They burn their houses down.

·

How heavy my mind is,
filled with the past.
Is there enough room
for the world to penetrate?
It must go somewhere,
it cannot simply sit on the surface—

.

Stars gleaming over the water.
The leaves piled, waiting to be lit.

.

Insight, my sister said.
Now it is here.
But hard to see in the darkness.

You must find your footing
before you put your weight on it.

SECOND WIND

I think this is my second wind,
my sister said. Very
like the first, but that
ended, I remember. Oh
what a wind that was, so powerful
the leaves fell off the trees.
I don't think so,
I said. Well, they were
on the ground, my sister said. Remember
running around the park in Cedarhurst,
jumping on the piles, destroying them?
You never jumped, my mother said.
You were good girls; you stayed where I put you.
Not in our heads,
my sister said. I put
my arms around her. What
a brave sister you are,
I said.

THE SETTING SUN

I.

I'm glad you like it, he said,
since it may be the last of its kind.
There was nothing to say;
in fact, it did seem the end of something.
It was a solemn moment.
We stood awhile in silence, staring at it together.

Outside the sun was setting,
the sort of pointed symmetry
I have always noticed.

If only I'd known, he said,
the effect of words.
Do you see how this thing has acquired weight and importance
since I spoke?

I could have done this long ago, he said,
and not wasted my time beginning over and over.

2 .

My teacher was holding a brush
but then I was holding a brush too—
we were standing together watching the canvas
out of the corners of which
a turbulent darkness surged; in the center
was ostensibly a portrait of a dog.
The dog had a kind of forced quality;
I could see that now. I have
never been much good with living things.
Brightness and darkness I do rather well with.
I was very young. Many things had happened
but nothing had happened
repeatedly, which makes a difference.
My teacher, who had spoken not a word, began to turn now
to the other students. Sorry as I felt for myself at that moment,
I felt sorrier for my teacher, who always wore the same clothes,
and had no life, or no apparent life,
only a keen sense of what was alive on canvas.
With my free hand, I touched his shoulder.
Why, sir, I asked, have you no comment on the work before us?
I have been blind for many years, he said,
though when I could see I had a subtle and discerning eye,
of which, I believe, there is ample evidence in my own work.
This is why I give you assignments, he said,

and why I question all of you so scrupulously.

As to my current predicament: when I judge from a student's

despair and anger he has become an artist,

then I speak. Tell me, he added,

what do you think of your own work?

Not enough night, I answered. In the night I can see my own soul.

That is also my vision, he said.

3.

I'm against
symmetry, he said. He was holding in both hands
an unbalanced piece of wood that had been
very large once, like the limb of a tree:
this was before its second life in the water,
after which, though there was less of it
in terms of mass, there was greater
spiritual density. Driftwood,
he said, confirms my view—this is why it seems
inherently dramatic. To make this point,
he tapped the wood. Rather violently, it seemed,
because a piece broke off.
Movement! he cried. That is the lesson! Look at these paintings,
he said, meaning ours. I have been making art
longer than you have been breathing
and yet my canvases have life, they are drowning
in life— Here he grew silent.
I stood beside my work, which now seemed rigid and lifeless.
We will take our break now, he said.

I stepped outside, for a moment, into the night air.
It was a cold night. The town was on a beach,
near where the wood had been.
I felt I had no future at all.
I had tried and I had failed.
I had mistaken my failures for triumphs.
The phrase *smoke and mirrors* entered my head.
And suddenly my teacher was standing beside me,
smoking a cigarette. He had been smoking for many years,
his skin was full of wrinkles.
You were right, he said, the way
instinctively you stepped aside.
Not many do that, you'll notice.
The work will come, he said. The lines
will emerge from the brush. He paused here
to gaze calmly at the sea in which, now,
all the planets were reflected. The driftwood
is just a show, he said; it entertains the children.
Still, he said, it is rather beautiful, I think,
like those misshapen trees the Chinese grow.
Pun-sai, they're called. And he handed me
the piece of driftwood that had broken off.
Start small, he said. And patted my shoulder.

4 .

Try to think, said the teacher,
of an image from your childhood.
Spoon, said one boy. Ah, said the teacher,
this is not an image. It is,
said the boy. See, I hold it in my hand
and on the convex side a room appears
but distorted, the middle taking longer to see
than the two ends. Yes, said the teacher, that is so.
But in the larger sense, it is not so: if you move your hand
even an inch, it is not so. You weren't there, said the boy.
You don't know how we set the table.
That is true, said the teacher. I know nothing
of your childhood. But if you add your mother
to the distorted furniture, you will have an image.
Will it be good, said the boy, a strong image?
Very strong, said the teacher.
Very strong and full of foreboding.

A SENTENCE

Everything has ended, I said.

What makes you say so, my sister asked.

Because, I said, if it has not ended, it will end soon

which comes to the same thing. And if that is the case,

there is no point in beginning

so much as a sentence.

But it is not the same, my sister said, this ending soon.

There is a question left.

It is a foolish question, I answered.

A CHILDREN'S STORY

Tired of rural life, the king and queen
return to the city, all the little princesses
rattling in the back of the car, singing the song of being:
I am, you are, he, she, it is—
But there will be
no conjugation in the car, oh no.
Who can speak of the future? Nobody knows anything about the future,
even the planets do not know.
But the princesses will have to live in it.
What a sad day the day has become.
Outside the car, the cows and pastures are drifting away;
they look calm, but calm is not the truth.
Despair is the truth. This is what
mother and father know. All hope is lost.
We must return to where it was lost
if we want to find it again.

A MEMORY

A sickness came over me
whose origins were never determined
though it became more and more difficult
to sustain the pretense of normalcy,
of good health or joy in existence—
Gradually I wanted only to be with those like myself;
I sought them out as best I could
which was no easy matter
since they were all disguised or in hiding.
But eventually I did find some companions
and in that period I would sometimes walk
with one or another by the side of the river,
speaking again with a frankness I had nearly forgotten—
And yet, more often we were silent, preferring
the river over anything we could say—
On either bank, the tall marsh grass blew
calmly, continuously, in the autumn wind.
And it seemed to me I remembered this place
from my childhood, though
there was no river in my childhood,
only houses and lawns. So perhaps
I was going back to that time
before my childhood, to oblivion, maybe
it was that river I remembered.

AFTERNOONS AND EARLY EVENINGS

The beautiful golden days when you were soon to be dying
but could still enter into random conversations with strangers,
random but also deliberate, so impressions of the world
were still forming and changing you,
and the city was at its most radiant, uncrowded in summer
though by then everything was happening more slowly—
boutiques, restaurants, a little wine shop with a striped awning,
once a cat was sleeping in the doorway;
it was cool there, in the shadows, and I thought
I would like to sleep like that again, to have in my mind
not one thought. And later we would eat polpo and saganaki,
the waiter cutting leaves of oregano into a saucer of oil—
What was it, six o'clock? So when we left it was still light
and everything could be seen for what it was,
and then you got in the car—
Where did you go next, after those days,
where although you could not speak you were not lost?

SONG

Leo Cruz makes the most beautiful white bowls;
I think I must get some to you
but how is the question
in these times

He is teaching me
the names of the desert grasses;
I have a book
since to see the grasses is impossible

Leo thinks the things man makes
are more beautiful
than what exists in nature

and I say no.
And Leo says
wait and see.

We make plans
to walk the trails together.
When, I ask him,
when? Never again:
that is what we do not say.

He is teaching me
to live in imagination:

a cold wind
blows as I cross the desert;
I can see his house in the distance;
smoke is coming from the chimney

That is the kiln, I think;
only Leo makes porcelain in the desert

Ah, he says, you are dreaming again

And I say then I'm glad I dream
the fire is still alive

ACKNOWLEDGMENTS

The American Scholar

Liberties

The New Yorker

The New York Review of Books

The Paris Review

The Threepenny Review

My continued thanks to Lisa Halliday.